TOTTENHAM at the DOUBLE

Ron Carlton-Gwilliam

TOTTENHAM at the DOUBLE

Ron Carlton-Gwilliam

First published in Great Britain as a softback original in 2022

Illustrated by Dennis Alveranga

Steve Perryman Illustrated by June Allan

Editing, design, typesetting and publishing by UK Book Publishing

www.ukbookpublishing.com

ISBN: 978-1-915338-42-6

Introduction

As I approached another significant landmark birthday I reflected on the many wonderful times that I have been fortunate to experience in my life. Having been a 'Spurs' supporter for well over sixty years, it will come as no surprise that, of all the sporting memories that come flooding back, nothing tops the 'Double' and that wonderful team of 1960-61. The more I reflected, the more I realised that we are, sadly, losing not only many of those fabulous players but also many of the fans, like myself, who turned out week after week to actually cheer them on to the greatest achievement in the club's history.

In those days the majority of 'Tottenham' supporters were also 'Tottenham' residents. But what were those players and the area of that time actually like? I soon realised that I was as qualified as anyone else still alive to answer those intriguing questions and hopefully leave a lasting record for future generations of fans through the everyday lives of a typical 'Tottenham' family and the exploits of their local heroes.

The following pages are my memories and experiences of not only those times but also some comparisons to what I believe was the nearest, most talented 'Spurs' side that might, just might, had one particular event not happened, have been able to emulate this wonderful feat. I am referring to the players of the early 80s.

Both sides had that essential mix of sheer guile and class mixed with power and determination. Think Danny Blanchflower, Cliff Jones, Les Allen and John White. Then think Glenn Hoddle, Tony Galvin, Ossie Ardiles and Ricky Villa. Think Dave

Mackay, Maurice Norman and Bobby Smith. Then think Steve Perryman, Graham Roberts and Garry Mabbutt, in my opinion, the last three great inspirational on-field 'Generals' to pull on the famous lilywhite shirt. Both of these two talented squads had one thing in common, they each had what would become the most successful and respected club captains of all-time in Danny Blanchflower and Steve Perryman, who would go on to become the most successful trophy-winning player in the history of the club and currently holds the record number of appearances.

Ron Carlton-Gwilliam

June Allan

Contribution from Steve Perryman MBE

I can recommend this book as having met the writer, his passion, matched by knowledge of his favourite subject (THFC) shine through every sentence of his story both verbally and by the written word.

I've learnt that real supporters are more than entitled to declare and prove their love for the Club as much as the most committed of us ex-players, especially the home-grown ones.

Ron's way of doing so is by sharing his exceptional in-depth knowledge and experiences of not only those heady seasons of the early 60s, 70s and 80s, but that of the area itself, the schools, factories, cinemas and social conditions of a bygone era.

We authors have to stick together, never just for the sake of it but also for our undying love for the mighty THFC. Ron's added comparisons of the squads of the early 60s and 80s feature many wonderful talents to hold forever strong in our memory.

Enjoy this thought-provoking book to add to your loyalty and support of our great Club.

Steve Perryman MBE
(An older one of our own)

Dedication

To my dad Alf (of whom, sadly, I have no memory), my mum Annie who, like so many women, was the glue that held my family together, my elder sister Pat and brother Alf, all sadly no longer with us and, not only to those members of that wonderful 'Spurs' team, who have now passed, but to those still surviving:

Thanks for the memories.

Lastly, to my son Karl, who has not only carried on the 'Tottenham family' tradition but, for the past 45 years, has shared with me the agonies and ecstasies of supporting the 'Spurs'.

Special thanks

To John Fennelly (Club Historian) for your encouragement and assistance. To Steve Perryman MBE for your kind contribution. Also, to Roy Beck, a relatively recent and considerably younger 'Super fan' acquaintance whose knowledge of all things relating to Tottenham Hotspur and devotion to the club is inspiring!

Spurs used a total of 17 players during the 1960-61 Double season:

The following 11 players were considered the first choice for their respective positions:

1. **Bill Brown** (Goalkeeper) Born: 8 Oct 1931 Arbroath/Scotland. Died: 30 Nov 2004 Simcoe/Canada
2. **Peter Baker** (Right Back) Born: 10 Dec 1931 Hampstead/London. Died: 27 Jan 2016 Hampstead
3. **Ron Henry** (Left Back) Born: 17 Aug 1934 Shoreditch/London. Died: 27 Dec 2014 Harpenden
4. **Danny Blanchflower** (Right Half) Born: 10 Feb 1926 Belfast/Ireland. Died: 9 Dec 1993 London
5. **Maurice Norman** (Centre Half) Born: 8 May 1934 Mulbarton/Norfolk
6. **Dave MacKay** (Left Half) Born: 14 Nov 1934 Edinburgh/Scotland. Died: 2 Mar 2015 Nottingham
7. **Cliff Jones** (Right Wing) Born: 7 Feb 1935 Swansea/Wales.
8. **John White** (Inside Right) Born: 28 Apr 1937 Musselburgh/Scotland. Died: 21 July 1964 Crews Hill
9. **Bobby Smith** (Centre Forward) Born: 22 Feb 1933 Lingdale/N Yorks. Died: 18 Sep 2010 Enfield
10. **Les Allen** (Inside Left) Born: 4 Sep 1937 Dagenham/Essex.
11. **Terry Dyson** (Left Wing) Born: 29 Nov 1934 Scarborough/Yorkshire.

The following six players were used when injury or tactical reasons dictated otherwise:

1. **John Hollowbread** (Goalkeeper) Born: 2 Jan 1934 Enfield. Died: 7 Dec 2007 Torrevieja/Spain
2. **Ken Barton** (Full Back) Born: 20 Sep 1937 Caernarfon/Wales. Died: 6 Sep 1982 Chester/England
3. **Tony Marchi** (Half Back) Born: 21 Jan 1933 Edmonton/London. Died: 15 Mar 2022 Chelmsford
4. **John Smith** (Wing Half/Inside Forward) Born: 4 Jan 1939 Shoreditch. Died: Feb 1988 Brent/London
5. **Terry Medwin** (Forward/Winger) Born: 25 Sep 1932 Swansea/Wales.
6. **Frank Saul** (Forward) Born: 23 Aug 1943 Canvey Island/Essex.

Bill Nicholson (Manager) Born: 26 Jan 1919 Scarborough/Yorkshire. Died: 23 Oct 2004 Hertfordshire

Correct at time of printing.

TOTTENHAM at the DOUBLE

There is a saying 'If you can remember the sixties you probably weren't there'. I do… and I was! As a matter of fact, I was also there in the fifties, 27 May 1952 to be precise. I was living in Tottenham at a time when Tottenham was a borough in the district of Middlesex. One year earlier, the local football team had become the champions of England for the first time in their history. Ten years later they would become the first team to complete the modern 'Double' of First Division Champions and FA Cup winners, which at the time, many people thought to be impossible.

This is the story of one fan's life and love affair with both the area and famous football club of that time. Throughout the following pages I'll share not only my memories of growing up in Tottenham, but also of the many fabulous Spurs players and some of the incredible matches they took part in both during and after the fabulous 'Double'.

My birth certificate shows that I was actually born in the Metropolitan Borough of Stoke Newington, a few miles south of Tottenham due to the fact that my mother, whilst heavily pregnant, had decided to visit one of my uncles (my mum's family were all from the Shoreditch area) and I took the opportunity to surprise him, my aunty and my mum by flooding their kitchen lino. Shortly afterwards, my mum and I were whisked off to Bearsted Memorial, the local Mothers' hospital. This was a Jewish hospital that had moved from Whitechapel in east London to a new site in the north of the city. The hospital was built with funds raised not only by poor Jews but many wealthy donors including Viscount Bearsted, after whose family the hospital was named, and had joined the NHS in 1948. While catering for some 80 per cent orthodox Jewish mothers, the hospital also admitted women of other faiths.

At this time my family, which comprised my father Alfred Charles, my mother Annie Elizabeth, my sister Patricia Anne and my brother, also Alfred Charles (the term Jnr not being in vogue then) had been residing at number 57 Scales Road, Tottenham, N17.

It's interesting to place on record that in the Spurs programme for the opening match of the 1952-53 season against West Bromwich Albion on 23 August, 'The Editor's Review and Spurs Gossip Of The Week' announced that the club had purchased a new playing field at Brookfield Lane, Cheshunt. The article went on to inform supporters that this new ground would be the permanent home of the club's nursery teams and that the ground was to be opened on Thursday September 4th when the "A" Team will meet Arsenal "A" in the Eastern Counties League which kicks off at 6pm. The price of admission would be one shilling for adults and six pence for boys. It's fascinating to note that in those days, as far as many football clubs were concerned, girls didn't watch football? Can you imagine the outcry that such a statement would have attracted these days? Being four days short of three months old, I could not possibly have known the importance that this new ground would play in my adult life, but more of that later.

Christmas and football during the 50s and 60s were always a special combination, more so for the men of the household. It was generally accepted that the women would stay home to cook the festive meal while the men went off to the local pub and then on to watch a football match. It may come as a surprise to many people today to know that at one time top-flight football was actually played on Christmas Day itself followed by a return match, often with the same opposition, on Boxing Day. I'm delighted to report that on my first-ever Christmas Day, seven months after being born, Spurs beat Middlesbrough 7-1 at White Hart Lane in the old First Division and followed it up with a 4-0 win in the return match two days later. What a pity that at that age I had no idea who Tottenham Hotspur were, let alone Middlesbrough! This was not strictly a Christmas Day/Boxing Day fixture as the return game was on 27 December which was what happened when Boxing Day would fall on a Sunday. For the record, Spurs have played 31 times on both the 25 and 26 December. Thirteen of these were in the old First Division and nine times in Division 2. The last time being during season 1958-59. Prior to these, Spurs played eight times in the Southern League Division 1 and once in the Football League South, immediately after WWII. The first ever recorded Christmas Day Spurs match was away to Millwall Athletic in the Southern League in season1896-97 which resulted in a 4-0 win.

Now I can't pretend that I took an instant interest in football. In fact, the first three years of my life are something of a blur which, in hindsight, could be described as a blessing in disguise because sadly, in March 1955, my mum became a widow. My dad, who was a tiler's mate, went to work one morning and never came home. Apparently he told a workmate that he "wasn't feeling too good" before collapsing and dying due to a thrombosis at the age of thirty-five, leaving my mum a single parent at the even younger age of thirty-three. From then on money was tight as these were days when insurance policies for many working-class families were an unaffordable luxury and self-employed workers had no company insurance or pension protection either. But happier days were to return for our family and before very long the 'Spurs' entered my life.

The first of these happier days began in early 1956 when the council re-housed us in a three-bedroom maisonette at number 49 Turner Avenue, N15, a relatively new estate just off West Green Road. This is where we lived for the next 14 years and would be the home where most of my happiest childhood memories would be made. During our time here, the Spurs would win the 'Double' in 1961, the FA Cup again in 1962, become the first British team to win a European trophy, the European Cup Winners' Cup, in 1963, the FA Cup again in 1967, and England would win the World Cup in 1966. The place seemed like a palace compared to our old house in Scales Road. When you entered the front door there was a hallway and to the right was a cupboard which Mum had converted to a coal-cupboard. Next to this was the kitchen and at the end of the hallway was the living-room which went completely across the rear of the property and where 'French doors' opened onto a tiny balcony. We never called it the living-room, it was always known as the front-room. This term appears to hark back to the days before the more modern flats and maisonettes were constructed. Houses were built so that the 'Best' or entertaining room would always be at the front of the house facing the road, with the kitchen always at the rear, leading to the back-yard (working-class families seldom had a back garden, it was nearly always a back-yard.) Up the stairs, to the left of the hallway, was a landing with a combined bathroom and toilet at the front of the property.

This was sheer luxury compared to the outside toilet at Scales Road. The bedroom next to it was shared by me and my brother Alf. The next bedroom was our sister Pat's. Mum's bedroom was at the rear and directly above the front room. There was a fireplace in the front room but none of the other rooms had any form of heating (central heating was good few years away), and in the winter they were freezing. At night we put coats on the beds to help keep us warm. Mum was terrified of thunder and lightning and whenever there was a storm she would unplug everything electrical and make us huddle together under the stairs. These maisonettes were all built on two levels. Ours was on the upper level. To reach it you had to go up four flights of stairs in the communal entrance and walk along the balcony; today it would be called the walkway. Our maisonette was the last of four and at the very end of the balcony. Also situated in the communal entrance, on each level, were the rubbish chutes. These chutes would one day cause me much anguish. But more of that in a while.

It would be fair to say that nothing particularly exciting or noteworthy comes to mind in the next few years of my life. But that would be both unfair and ungrateful to my mother who continued to provide a loving, safe and disciplined home life to us three kids. At a time when there was no Social Security as we know it today, she often had two jobs at a time. I'm sure that for my mother every day of those years and the months immediately after my father's death were filled with mud, sweat and tears. I can only hope that her daughter and two football-mad sons made it clear how much we loved and appreciated everything she did for us.

Going to a football match in the 60s was still pretty much the same as it was in the 50s and pre-second World War days and light years away from the modern-day experience. Instead of the fashion today of thousands of fans flocking outside the ground looking like 'Reserves' or 'Subs' with replica shirts or even full kits with numbers and names printed on the back, supporters then wore everyday clothes adorned with scarves and rosettes. These were the days before a club shop was even envisaged. Every match in all four top divisions of the football league then, kicked off at 3pm on Saturday. The streets around the ground would be filled with individual vendors selling scarves, rosettes and badges. Programmes could be purchased from the 'Official' programme sellers dressed in their smart uniform and cap. There were a good number of 'Pirate' programme sellers and, of course, the shady looking ticket touts. Food outlets were few and far between, and three of the most popular sights and smells were of roasted hot chestnuts sold from roadside braziers, monkey-nut sellers and Bovril. Close by the ground is Warmington House, a Grade II listed building, which for many years was the home of the 'Spurs Supporters Club'. Inside the ground a red cinder track surrounded the playing area and on both the East and West stand perimeter walls were placed letters of the alphabet which corresponded to the other fixtures of the day printed in the programme. These were used to inform supporters of the half-time and full-time scores in those other matches. For instance, alongside the letter 'A' which might be Burnley vs Everton for example, numbers would be placed. The home side's score would be on top with the away team below. This system was devised in the days of limited communication facilities. Apart from the seated areas around the ground, there were no such things as 'Executive' boxes. The only, and most important, two boxes were the 'Director's box', of course, and the wooden box that many small kids would bring onto the terraces for them to stand on! Can you imagine being allowed to bring these into a ground today, let alone the famous 'Rattle'? The match-day programmes, for many years, were printed by Thomas Knight & Sons of Hoddesdon.

Tottenham in the 50s and 60s was a very different place to the area of today. The most popular way to reach the ground was by the 649, 659 or 679 trolley buses in the 50s or the 149, 259 or 279 buses, as they became, in the 60s. The more exciting mode of transport, if you were a kid, was by train from Seven Sisters Station, via the entrance in West Green Road, to White Hart Lane. It's worth mentioning that in those days there was no Victoria Line underground station at Seven Sisters. If you were travelling from the Manor House area in the 60s, you could also use the 'Football Special' buses which for a 6d fare took you non-stop to the ground.

Interestingly, all those buses would pass close to another hospital that would play a part in my early life. Sadly, the 'Prince of Wales General Hospital' situated at the junction of Tottenham High Road, Tottenham Green and Tynemouth Road is now no longer functioning, but the Georgian building, at least, still remains and has since been converted to apartments. The most striking aspect of the hospital building was the semi-circular white façade (which has thankfully been retained) proudly displaying the 'Prince of Wales' feathers. It was here that I was rushed with a case of acute appendicitis in 1959. Prior to this (the year I cannot now recall) I was taken there to have my tonsils removed and whilst waiting to be admitted a hospital worker or possibly surgeon dressed in a white gown and cap emerged from the operating area with a young boy about my age unconscious in his arms. The boy had a large rubber weight clamped to his tongue which was used in those days to stop people from swallowing that appendage. The sight of this was enough to send me into hysterics and begging my mum to take me home, which she did, but not before she had verbally laid into the hospital staff for allowing me to witness this distressing scene and having now to try and placate a terrified son. Sometime after, and with great persuasion, another date was set for my operation. Another interesting fact was that it was also here in 1986 the BBC filmed Dennis Potter's 'The Singing Detective'.

Further north along Tottenham High Road during 1958 and 1959, Spurs were busy recruiting some of the players that would ultimately become the idols of my youth. February 1958 saw Cliff Jones sign from Swansea Town. In March 1959 he was joined by Dave Mackay from Heart of Midlothian and October 1959 saw the arrival of John White from Falkirk. These three giants of the game joined Danny Blanchflower, Maurice Norman and Bobby Smith, who between them formed half the legendary 'Double' winning team.

Now, at eight years of age, there were about to be two significant events, one exciting and one life-changing, to recall from my childhood. The exciting one was the start of what would turn out to be the greatest-ever season in the history of Tottenham Hotspur Football Club. The life-changing one was that it was discovered that I was completely deaf in my left ear. It would appear that in those days there was little that could be done for my condition, and because a hearing aid was of no use to me I was destined to endure years of people, at various times, asking 'are you deaf or stupid?'. There seemed little point in trying to explain which of these ailments was to blame for the particular situation in question. Happy days!

I'm ashamed to admit that I cannot remember the exact date or even the opposition for my first visit to White Hart Lane. Only that it was a hot sunny day and the visitors wore claret and blue shirts and white shorts, suggesting that it was either Aston Villa, Burnley or West Ham United. I can remember being in the lower East stand with my brother Alf, who was four years older than me. I spent the last half-hour or so sitting on the terracing, hot and bothered, asking 'how much longer before we can go home?' and my brother giving me that age-old precise estimate of 'not long' before adding 'now shut it!'. On the way home my brother, who was never big on patience, informed me that he was 'never taking me again'. Fortunately, it was not the first or the last time that he would lie to me and over the next few years we would spend many a Saturday afternoon at 'The Lane' standing on the 'shelf' with our older cousin Ray who first introduced my brother to the joys of watching the 'Spurs'. As time went on the three of us were joined by more of our cousin Ray's friends, Bob, Tony and Albert. Tony was a right moody bugger. He had this superstition that if he was late or got distracted and missed seeing the player kicking-off the match, then Spurs would lose. On the rare occasions that Spurs were playing badly, or worse still, losing, you would look round and Tony had pissed off without saying a word to anyone. One of our match-day practices was to buy an extra programme and tear the names out, which would then be folded and each of us would put a shilling or so in the kitty before choosing a name for the 'first goal scorer'. In the mid-sixties everyone, of course, was hoping to draw Jimmy Greaves. One match-day our cousin Ray, who was a bit of a joker, picked the 'Golden ticket'. Shortly before the kick-off he suddenly announced, "I can guarantee that Greavsie's not going to score today". We all wondered if perhaps he had heard that Jimmy Greaves was injured and that the news had not been made public yet. "Why not?" someone asked. "Because I've got him in my pocket," replied Ray as he chuckled for all he was worth. The team in those days always came out to the strains of 'Macnamara's band'.

Despite the difficulties experienced by our family, my childhood was a happy one. Mum continued to provide a warm, clean home and we never went hungry. Tottenham in those days was a safe area to live and the only warning most of us kids were given when we went out to play was 'watch out for dirty old men in raincoats'. The only other warning our mum gave us was when she would jokingly say "be careful, if you come home dead, I'll kill you".

When we went out to play, it comprised mainly of football and cricket games on the grassed areas within the estate, or riding bikes and roller skating around the estate roads. There were very few cars in those days and these roads were mainly used by service vehicles such as milkmen, coalmen and delivery vans. Neither Alf nor me were particularly interested in riding bikes, which was probably for the best for a couple of good reasons. The first was that bikes were still a considerable outlay for our mum, and the second being that apart from having to lug a bike up and down the communal stairs there was no room in our house to store them. The only other option would have been to leave it outside on the balcony. However, even though it would have been perfectly safe, the Council, in those days, were very strict about anything blocking or being left on the balconies. But football was a different matter. We once had a 'Frido' football. This was a vinyl ball which was orange in colour and covered in small pimples. They were launched in 1959 and endorsed by the great Stanley Matthews (yet to be knighted); it was our pride and joy, for a while at least. You see, these balls were easily damaged especially if used on hard surfaces. One particular day the ball got a small split in it and started to deflate. Not having bikes, we also didn't have any puncture repair kits, but Alf had a brilliant idea. He took one of Mum's old cutlery knives and held it over the lighted gas hob. When the knife was hot enough, he placed it over the area of the ball where it had split and melted the surrounding vinyl and spread it like butter over the split. When the vinyl cooled it had sealed the split and, with a borrowed bicycle-pump, we were able to re-inflate the ball. Genius!

There were of course the two local parks, namely, Downhills Park and Lordship Lane Recreation Ground. The nearest of these to my home was Downhills Park, which had an entrance at the junction of West Green Road and Phillip Lane. This park stretched some considerable distance to the other entrance in Downhills Park Road. On the other side of Downhills Park Road was the smaller entrance to Lordship Lane 'Rec' as we called it, the main entrance being in Lordship Lane itself and directly opposite Waltheof Avenue, where in 1980, I would buy my first home under the Conservatives' 'Homesteading' Scheme. The jewel in the crown of the 'Rec' was the children's traffic area. This was a miniaturised road system complete with traffic lights, crossings and Halt signs, which were used before the now familiar 'Give Way' signs, and where local kids could gain road sense and learn to ride their bicycles safely. It was here that the Royal Society for the Prevention of Accidents would conduct the Cycling Proficiency Test, which served as the minimum recommended standard for cycling on British roads.

Other forms of entertainment consisted of swimming pools such those at Tottenham baths or, in the summer months, the open-air Lido in Lordship Lane. The Cinema was of course the main form of family entertainment in the evenings or at weekends, with television a relatively new and scarce addition to the home. Even when televisions did become more accessible, many working-class families were unable to afford to buy one outright. Like many other families we rented a TV set. One of my childhood memories had escaped me until my mum reminded me of it many years later. It appears that when I was small, she had been unable to keep up the rental payments and the TV set was taken away. Eventually Mum was in a position to afford to rent another one and she told me that on the day they installed it I was sitting on the front-room floor and looked up at her and said, "They're not going to take this one away, are they, Mum?" Mum said that it always brought a lump to her throat whenever she remembered that day. With regards to cinemas, there were a good selection in the area such as Bruce Grove, the 'Florida' in Tottenham High Road, the 'Imperial' in West Green Road and the 'Curzon' at Ducketts Common. But the two main cinemas that my friends and family frequented were the 'Palace' in Tottenham High Road, almost opposite the police station, and the 'ABC Ritz' at Turnpike Lane. It might surprise many people today to know that in those days the national anthem was always played at the end of the film, or programme, as it was called then. Mum always made us stand as did everybody else and it was frowned upon for anyone to leave before it finished.

As I got older one TV programme in particular stands out in my mind as, in a funny way, it highlights the difficulties my hearing defect was to have on my life. The programme in question was called 'The Forest Rangers'. This was a Canadian television series that ran from 1963 to 1965 and as the title suggests it centred on life in the Canadian outback. In one episode there was an argument between two of the main characters resulting in one of them storming off. Mum had been watching the programme with me but had to pop in and out of the room from time to time and came back just as this happened and said "Where is he going?". I told her, "He said he's going to shoot someone's rabbits." This made no sense to Mum in relation to the storyline. But all became clear in the next scene when the guy in question was paddling like mad in a canoe through a fast-flowing river. My mum looked at me and laughed. "He's shooting the rapids, you silly sod." At least this was a case of being 'deaf' not 'stupid'. Mum and me would both still chuckle years later whenever we remembered this incident. Happy days.

My entire school days during the 50s and 60s were spent at three schools: Seven Sisters JMI, South Grove, and Downhills Secondary Modern. In those days we walked everywhere. From my home in Turner Avenue en route to Seven Sisters JMI School, I would turn right into West Green Road, past the Fountain Public House, then right into Braemar Road and under the railway bridge into Seaford Road. One particular day I was walking with another kid from our estate when a fire engine, bells ringing like the clappers, flew past us in the direction of the school. Now I didn't know anything about the power of positive thinking at that age, but I turned to the other kid and said "I wish it was the school that was on fire" and to my surprise and delight when we got there it was! Apparently, there was a fire in the staff room and the school was closed for the day. South Grove School required a short walk along Elmer Road, turning left at the Off Licence on the corner into Avenue Road, then left again at a barber's shop that was, coincidently, called 'Ron's', into Newsam Avenue leading to South Grove. My time at South Grove was curtailed early when the school was merged with what, at one time, was the County School later re-named Downhills Central. By the time I started in the first year of South Grove, my brother, being four years older than me, was in the fourth and last year of his school days there. I still remember when he warned me which kids to watch out for. But one name in particular frightened the life out of me. He pointed at this huge beast of a kid and said, "Watch out for him, that's Spor." I still to this day do not know if that was how it was spelt, but I nearly crapped myself and I certainly knew how that was spelt and how it would have smelt if he ever came after me! Downhills Secondary Modern as it became at the time of the merger was situated alongside the Town Hall, Fire Station and Public Baths in Town Hall Approach. Walking to Downhills involved turning right into West Green Road, then left into Beaconsfield Road before again turning right into Clyde

Road at the junction with Clyde Circus. I'm afraid to report that I achieved very little during my school days apart from the basic 'three Rs', reading, riting and rithmetic as they were then known, owing to the fact that they were pronounced by dropping the 'W' and 'A' from writing and arithmetic respectively. What a great way to start a kid's education…let's confuse the little buggers. Well this little bugger decided: "If you can't be bothered to stick to the Queen's English then I ain't either." It was at Downhills that I met my first love (after football) and her name was Barbara. I will keep her surname to myself so as not to embarrass her if she or somebody that knows her should, just by chance, read this book. All I will say is she lived in Vincent Road, just off West Green Road. Sadly, the romance didn't last long but I still have fond memories of Barbara. My three closest pals at school were Floris (a Cypriot), Tony and George (The Bullfrog) as we called him on account of his booming gruff laugh. Probably the most memorable other moment of my school-days when at Downhills involved football and my favourite teacher Mr Ted Say. During one sports lesson it was decided to play a game of football in the tarmac playground. My team were being soundly beaten and, not being a very good loser, I decided to take the ankles of a lad on the other team as he flew past me for the umpteenth time. The next thing I was aware of was being punched in the jaw from behind. I turned to see Mr Say, who was refereeing the game and who had delivered the blow! "Don't ever, do that again," he said. In those days it never occurred to anyone to report a teacher for such an action. Not that I would anyway, for Mr Say was the most enjoyable and inspiring teacher I had ever encountered. Besides, I deserved it!

I left school to join the grown-up world in the summer of 1967, not long after Spurs had beaten Chelsea 2-1 in the FA Cup Final with a team that included yet more of my idols, namely, Pat Jennings,

Cyril Knowles, Jimmy Greaves and Alan Gilzean. Happy days just kept on coming.

My introduction into the world of work was thanks to the General Post Office, or GPO as it was then known. I became an 'Internal' messenger boy and I had to report to King Edward Building, St Martins-le-Grand, which involved a short route 41 bus ride from my home in West Green Road followed by a London Underground journey on the Piccadilly line from Turnpike Lane Station to St Paul's in London. I earned seven pounds a week.

In the days before Wood Green Shopping Centre or an easy 15-minute underground journey from Seven Sisters Station on the Victoria Line to Oxford Circus, West Green Road, from the junction with Lawrence Road to Seven Sisters corner and Tottenham High Road, was the main shopping street for local residents. Pretty much everything you could need for day-to-day living could be bought here. Virtually all the shops in those days were independent or family run. Fruit and veg could be bought from Pontins (no connection with the holiday camp empire) and where one of the men working there would take pleasure in amazing kids, myself included, by appearing to make a tomato or some other round edible object come out of your ear. I once asked him if he could do it from out of my left ear in the hope that it might have been the cause of my affliction, but alas, no joy there. There was a hardware shop, the name of which escapes me now, where we used to buy Pink or Blue paraffin for the heater, as well as candles, string, matches and all sorts of brooms, brushes, dusters and the like. I can still recall the smell of these items today and loved the fact that it had a hard wooden floor which was liberally sprinkled with sawdust. There was David Grieg's the grocers and a small supermarket where you could, for the first time, take a shopping basket round, pick your own items and present it to the shop owner at the till (very modern for the times). There was the Swap Shop which sold all sorts of second-hand items such as guitars, air pistols, books etc, and as the name suggest, would accept articles in exchange for something the customer wanted, or allow the customer to pay for the item on a weekly payment plan. On the left-hand corner as you approached Tottenham High Road was a store called Rudds that sold amongst other things Dinky toys and Hornby train sets. Further back and on the opposite side of West Green Road was Woolworth's, where my childhood aspirations of being a modern-day Artful Dodger would start and finish in the space of just a few minutes. This is yet another of those memories where I'm afraid I cannot be sure of exactly how old I was at the time, but I guess I would be somewhere between seven and nine. I can, however, remember the incident as clear as if it were only yesterday. The objects of my desire were small plastic figures of the 101 Dalmatians. I had seen them when I had gone into the store a few days earlier with my mum. On the day in question, I can remember sifting through the figures and decided to put three of them in my trouser pocket. Even though, in my younger days, everybody called me Ronnie, I was definitely no Ronnie Biggs or Ronnie Kray. And even I had worked out that I was never going to fit in another 98, and decided to walk out of the store. No sooner had I stepped onto the pavement than I felt a hand on my shoulder and a man's voice saying, "Just a minute, young man." I froze. I never did find out if he was a store-detective or just a shop worker, and I wasn't taken back into the store as would happen today. I was told to hand over the items I had stolen and then asked for my name and address. Now, I remember that my mum always described me as a little sod as a kid, but I was certainly not in the same league as a lot of the other local 'Herberts' as mum used to call them. I knew for a fact that many of them could reel-off a couple false names and addresses without blinking. I, on the other hand, could barely give this bloke my correct name and address without stammering. Then he said that someone would come round to our house soon to have a word with my mum. For the next week at least, I lived in absolute fear that someone would pay us a visit. Every time there was a knock on the door, especially in the evenings, when Mum would say "Now who can that be at this time", my stomach would knot-up and the cheeks of my arse would decide to close ranks. I can only imagine that whoever this bloke was he probably realised that I was terrified and could be pretty sure he had taught me a lesson. Nobody ever did come round and Mum never found out.

The Jewel in the crown of this shopping experience was Wards Stores, situated on the corner of Seven Sisters Road and Tottenham High Road. Wards was upmarket…the Harrods of the area, at least that's how it appeared to me, having never even heard of or seen inside the luxury London store. The nearest comparable store was Burgess's department store situated between Reform Row and Scotland Green. The most amazing thing about Wards, apart from all the lovely items they sold, was the fascinating payment system they employed. When you purchased your item or items, the shop assistant would write the items and total price on a duplicated ticket and place the ticket along with your money in a metal canister which had a screw top. This was then screwed to a metal lid that was attached to a zip wire that whisked the container up towards the ceiling where a cashier's office was situated. There was a zip line going to each of the counters in the store. The ticket was checked, stamped and the receipt portion along with any change due would then be placed back into the container and sent back down to the counter. It was worth the visit just to watch these canisters flying backwards and forwards.

For many years, weekends for me consisted of shopping in the morning with Mum on Saturday before coming home to play out with the other kids on the estate or going to watch the 'Spurs' with my brother in the afternoon. There was of course no professional football played on Sunday, only the usual amateur league matches in the mornings. From midday onwards Mum would be busy preparing and cooking Sunday dinner. I can't vouch for every other family in Tottenham at that time, but in our house meal times consisted of breakfast, dinner-time and tea-time. I have often had people disputing our chosen terminology but as far as I'm concerned you took your 'dinner' money to school on Mondays and schools employed 'dinner' ladies. So, if it was good enough for the Education authorities, it was good enough for us. There was no such thing as lunch and supper, they were for the posh knobs.

Mum had three main vices. The first was she smoked Guards cigarettes, or 'fags' as she called them, which were made by a company called Carreras which later merged with Rothmans. The packet was red, white and black and had a picture of a guardsman in his tunic, trousers and Busby. Considering the lengths that are in place today to discourage smoking, it might amaze many people to know that cigarettes could be bought loose or even from machines that were fixed to walls outside some shops. Surprisingly, despite Mum smoking all her life, none of us kids took up the habit.

The second was she liked a bottle of Guinness whilst she was preparing and cooking the Sunday roast dinner. In those days, before the rise of aluminium cans, pretty much every drink was bottled. Another of my most vivid and amusing early memories involved a weekend and bottles. It was rare for us to go for a day out, but one Saturday Mum took me and my brother to Hyde

Park in London. We had had a nice time and Mum bought us each a bottle of pop as we called it then from a man in a kiosk in the park. These were before the days when Coca-Cola ruled the world. It was common practice for shops and businesses to charge a deposit, which could be refunded when the bottles were returned. It was usually only about one or two pence on each bottle. Many people simply couldn't be bothered to take the empty bottles back and would just leave them lying around or throw them in bins. Mum decided me and my brother could earn ourselves some pocket money by running around the park and collecting up as many bottles as we could find. I think it was on about our third visit that the bloke in the kiosk refused to give us the money as it clearly wasn't us that had bought them all. We went and told Mum and she marched up to the kiosk and verbally laid into the miserable sod. Now, I'm no expert, but in law he might well have had a point, but he wasn't legally represented and we had Mum. You could say the bloke lost his bottle, but in fact he gained his bottles and we got our money. If it were a football match it would have been possibly the first-ever Tottenham Women 1 Hyde Park Men 0.

Mum's third little vice was a weekly flutter on the football pools. The four main pools companies at the time were Littlewoods, Vernon's, Cope's and Zetters. I can remember that in those days the top prize or 'Jackpot' was £75,000, which doesn't sound very much compared to the millions on offer today for things like the National Lottery, but you have to remember that the average house price in 1960 was £2,530. No ordinary working-class person really dreamed of being a 'Millionaire' as that would be like someone today hoping to become a 'Billionaire'. Mum would always say, 'Just wait till we win that Jackpot, we'll be rich!' The only money she ever won was ten shillings, which came through the post in the form of a postal order.

In the sixties, working class people very rarely went out to restaurants for a meal. For a start, there was nothing like the amount and choice of restaurants or fast-food outlets that there are today. The most common and popular choice to be had was a trip to the fish & chip shop or chippy on a Friday evening where you would carry home your fish & chips wrapped up in old newspapers. There was of course one other favourite treat to be had where you could sit down to eat, and I am referring to the Pie & Mash shop. Depending on where you lived, you had the choice of either Manze's or Cooke's. Ours was Manze's in Seven Sisters Road, not far from the Woodberry Tavern Public House. Mum's favourite was the eels, jellied or stewed; we three kids preferred the pies and mash served with liquor, which of course is merely a parsley sauce and nothing to do with alcohol. The green colour of the sauce still puts people off even today. In those days it was common for the eels to be swimming about in a large tray of water at the front of the shop and the staff would take them out and chop them up as they were needed – talk about fresh food. This practice has of course long since stopped for obvious reasons. Now, you might notice that I have referred to it as the Pie & Mash shop, not restaurant. It was and still is a shop and not a restaurant – we working-class Londoners know our place! Apart from the food served in these establishments, I found the whole place including the seats and tables fascinating and still do to this day. The walls were always beautifully tiled with large mirrors, and the seats were like wooden church pews with high backs, whilst the table tops were white marble on cast iron legs. Not many survive today but I am extremely fortunate to live near Waltham Abbey where Tony's Pie & Mash shop still provides the same experience. Happy days.

Tottenham was a hive of industry during the 50s and 60s, with a vast amount of companies such as Gestetners, the world-famous stencil duplicator company in Broad Lane, which, at one time, was the largest employer in the area and where my mum was later to work and meet my step-father Cliff in 1966. Two years later their marriage resulted in the birth of a baby boy named Robert, who completed our family. The Tottenham Hale area was home to a number of companies such as Harris Lebus, Eagle Pencil and Lorrileux & Bolton, the ink manufacturers where I worked in the colour department in the mid-70s. My brother-in-law Mick had managed to get me a job there. I worked at the factory quite happily until being sacked for poor time-keeping. At the time the company had two shifts, early and late, the early starting at 6am and here, for me, lay the problem. Many companies in those days required you to clock-on and this was done by taking a piece of card with your name printed on and placing it in a slot attached to a large clock then pulling a handle. When you were on-time it stamped the time in black ink, if you were late it would stamp the time in red. My card was often dual coloured and this eventually led to my dismissal. Not so much 'Happy days'. Added to these companies were Cannon Rubber in Tottenham High Road, the Ever Ready Battery Company in St Anns Road, as was the Oceana Laundry Company, not to mention the Wonderloaf Bakery in White Hart Lane. Closest to my home in Turner Avenue was Lentheric, the perfumes and fragrances company situated in Lawrence Road and was perhaps most famously remembered for its 'Tweed' brand. The most gruesome of all the job opportunities in the area could be gained in the 'Slaughter House' in Summerhill Road. Makes the Pie & Mash shop eels seem tame by comparison.

Most Spurs supporters know only too well the history of the White Hart Public House and the reason for the name of the ground etc, but there are two other well-known pubs adjacent to the stadium, namely The Corner Pin, which is situated on the corner of Park Lane and only a few yards away from the Bell and Hare. It was common to see a few of the Spurs players enjoying a few drinks in the Bell and Hare after training at the ground during the week. A few hundred yards further north is Paxton Road, where the turnstiles to the north stand were situated. Just a few paces along Paxton Road was a Salvation Army Hall and it was here that one of my funniest match-day memories occurred. Running along the side of the Salvation Army Hall was an alleyway, at the end of which was a brick wall. It was possible to clamber over this wall and gain entry to the ground. Not surprisingly, it was because of this that a police officer would be stationed on match days. I remember one particular Saturday when I was in my early teens, myself and two of my pals, Floris and Tony, had arrived for a match. Tony, who knew full well why the policeman was there, decided to be a bit cheeky and stopped by the alleyway and started to peer over the policeman's shoulder and said out loud, "I wonder where that leads to." Without a moment's hesitation and delivered with a deadpan expression the policeman replied, "Tottenham Magistrates Court, 10 o'clock Monday morning, now hop it." They don't make coppers like that anymore. Classic.

Many people when looking back to their childhood often say that the sun always seemed to shine, but of course it didn't. When the weather was lousy there was little option for kids in the 50s and 60s except to occupy themselves indoors by playing games. These games must seem very boring to kids of today. In many homes there were the traditional board games such as Monopoly and Snakes and Ladders, for example. Chess or Draught sets and Dart boards were also very popular. But in our house my brother and me had hours of fun with just some toy soldiers, elastic bands and a pack of cards. Before I explain a number of the games we devised, I think I should explain why I rarely include my sister Pat in our play times. You see my sister was ten years older than me so from the time I was five years of age my sister would be fifteen and worked all week. By the time I was eight she was courting her boyfriend Mick whom she later went on to marry and set up home together. Pat was the best big sister you could wish to have and as we got older the age gap narrowed and we grew closer than ever until she sadly passed away in April 2020. Now, back to those games. One game we played involved each of us setting up a number of soldiers on opposite sides of the room and taking turns to fire elastic bands at each other's soldiers until one or the other's had all been wiped out. As a result of this game, we both became expert shots and could hit a fly or spider on the ceiling from across the room. I'm impressed that I can still do this today at least eight times out of ten. One game we devised with a pack of cards was a football game which involved shuffling the pack before counting out 30 cards face down and discarding the rest. Then each of us would choose a team from a number of teams written down on folded pieces of paper. We would then turn over one card at a time each until an ace came up which would be a 'Goal'. If a 'Jack' came up that would be a 'Penalty'. You then had to turn over two more cards and if they added up to 11 you had scored. If they didn't, you had missed the penalty. We often played the FA Cup competition through to the Final etc. The other game we played was horse racing. This was done by removing all four aces which were the horses. We would then shuffle all the cards and place eight cards face down lengthwise in a line on the table. These were the furlongs. We then lined up the aces face-up side by side behind the first furlong. After choosing one of the horses, each one of us would turn over one card at a time from the pack. If a diamond card came up you moved the corresponding ace up one furlong etc, until one of the horses reached and passed the last furlong. The beauty of this game is you had no idea which cards would be turned over or how many of one suit was face-down in the furlong line.

Having already discussed a number of the indoor games that me and my brother played as kids, there was no greater game than Subbuteo! This was the best Christmas present I ever got and can still remember the sheer elation I felt when I unwrapped my first set. I know that today's electronic versions with life-like players, crowd scenes and scoreboards are so very realistic, but there is no comparison to the tactile playing figures, goals and pitches of Subbuteo. The game was known as 'Flick to Kick' and the level of skill some players could achieve cannot be matched (no pun intended) by the control pad generation. I still today have two large plastic tubs full in my loft. Sadly, that much loved first set isn't one of them. The reason why is still a painful memory in more ways than one. As I stated previously, I was never a good loser, and one particular day Alf and me were playing a match in the front room and I started to get quite ratty. My brother, as you might recall me mentioning, not being big on patience, was starting to get pretty pissed off. The result was that 'Flick to Kick' soon became 'Quick to Hit' with me on the receiving end. But worse was to come. Our mum, who was in the kitchen at the time, and upon hearing the commotion once too often, snapped. She marched into the room, scooped up the pitch, players, goals, ball, every last bit and marched out the front door, along the balcony of our maisonettes, to the communal rubbish chutes and dumped the lot. I just stood there, mouth open, lips quivering and tears welling up in my eyes. "You won't be arguing over that again, will you?" she said as she came back and closed the door behind her. I couldn't reply even if I wanted to. When she left the room, I got another clump from my brother. This one, I decided, was best suffered in silence. Years later, I realised that it must also have been a painful experience for my mum, as these sets were not a small outlay for a single parent of three kids. Happy days were to return once more when the following Christmas Mum bought me a replacement set with the warning "You know where that's going if you two start again". She got the biggest kiss ever.

Among the famous people that had been both born and living in Tottenham in the sixties was Paul Trevillion, an artist, who was born in Love Lane in 1934. Paul started his career by sketching Spurs players whilst himself standing on the shelf as a boy. He would later go on to have a weekly feature in the 'Tottenham and Edmonton Herald' and would probably be most remembered for his depiction of 'Roy of the Rovers'. The second was Dave Clark who was born in Phillip Lane in 1942 and fronted the 'Dave Clark 5' pop group. The 'Band', as they would now be described, would appear regularly at the 'Royal' dance hall a few yards away from the 'Palace' cinema and where in 1969 I was to meet my first wife and the mother of my eldest two children, Emma-Jane and Karl.

Possibly one the most famous and important people in the history of Tottenham Hotspur Football Club to be born in Tottenham must surely be Arthur Rowe on 1 September 1906. Arthur Rowe, of course, was the first manager to guide the 'Spurs' to the first of the club's only two League Championships in 1951.The great Bill Nicholson having been born in Yorkshire, Arthur was a true Tottenham born and bred hero and, in my opinion, much under-appreciated.

You will by now have clearly gathered that most of my memories of Tottenham in the sixties are happy ones. But 21 July 1964 was not only one of the saddest in the history of Tottenham Hotspur Football Club but also served to strengthen my mum's fear of thunder and lightning. On the day in question, the great John

White was struck and killed by lightning at the age of 27 whilst sheltering under a tree at Crews Hill Golf club in Enfield. John White was possibly the greatest inside forward that has ever played for the club. Some of the older supporters would tell me that before John there was a player called Tommy Harmer who was nicknamed 'Harmer the Charmer' and was considered the greatest of his time and that it was difficult to choose between the two. I never got to see Tommy Harmer, but I did see John White and he was without doubt the most skilful player I had ever seen, until Glenn Hoddle came along. I now find myself in the same position as those older supporters in having to try and choose between these two superb players. Since then there has been the 'wonderful' Ossie Ardiles. But for me, John White and Glenn Hoddle take some beating.

Having drifted in and out of a variety of different jobs and workplaces as a young man including postman, window cleaning, a bakery and tailoring, I found myself working alongside my brother-in-law at the printing company from which, as previously documented, I was dismissed in 1975. The timing of this incident couldn't have been worse as my wife was heavily pregnant with our first child Emma-Jane. It was clearly apparent that I needed a job, and fast. Having no qualifications and no driving licence, my choices were limited. I found myself passing Manor House in Seven Sisters Road, which was the Leaside headquarters of London Transport, when I saw the sign outside which stated 'Bus Conductors wanted'. I ventured inside and just over an hour later I came out with a piece of paper instructing me to report to Chiswick Works on 11th August for four weeks' training after which I would be assigned to Tottenham garage in Phillip Lane. Little did I know then that I would spend the next 40 years of my working life on the buses, during which time I would go on to gain promotion to Inspector and Area Manager.

Many people over 50 years of age will remember when wages were paid weekly in cash in a sealed brown envelope (hence the term pay packet) which was discontinued by London Transport in 1976.The staff were required to open a bank account into which your wages would be paid. I duly went into the nearest bank to the garage which was Barclays at the junction with Tottenham High Road and Broad Lane. At the time of my new employment, we were living at number 24a Etherley road N15 which was a damp ground-floor flat in a terraced house. Soon after the council re-housed us in a brand new ground-floor flat which was very exciting. The only downside was that we had to move to Walthamstow. This made getting to and from Tottenham garage for early and late shifts extremely difficult as I still didn't drive and couldn't afford to run a car even if I could. It was while living here that my son Karl was born in 1977 and that same year I was finally able to purchase a season ticket for the first time as a number of disgruntled supporters had decided not to renew theirs after Spurs' recent relegation. During our stay here I was privileged to play for Tottenham. Unfortunately the word that followed Tottenham wasn't 'Hotspur' but 'Garage' ah well, almost 'Happy days'. In early 1980 our family's fortunes took a second turn for the better. My dear mum had, without our knowledge, put our names down in the hope of being eligible to purchase a house under the Conservatives 'Homesteading' scheme which only required a £5 deposit. To our delight we were indeed lucky enough to be selected and a few months later we returned to Tottenham and moved into number 8 Waltheof Avenue N17. These houses were, in general, in a poor state of repair and also in need of modernisation. Ours, which was boarded up and barely habitable, was no exception. The property still had an outside toilet, as did our old house in Scales Road in the 50s. In the next few years with two small children and still no driving licence, I embarked on regular journeys with the kids to Brookfield Lane,

Cheshunt, Tottenham Hotspur's training ground. This involved taking a route 243 bus from Lordship Lane to Tottenham High Road and then a route 279 bus to Cheshunt. This was a long journey which on some occasions involved alighting at Waltham Cross and taking another 279 bus onto Brookfield Lane. The bus stopped opposite the White Horse Public House in Flamstead End Road, which has long since gone, and, as I write, is now a Tesco Express. Then followed a long walk along Brookfield Lane itself. In those days it was possible to simply walk in and wander around the various practice pitches and either stand or sit down on the touchlines and watch the players going through their routines. There were no burly presidential-style security guards with dark glasses. No bags were searched or families frisked like today etc. Over the next five years or so my kids met and had photos taken with the likes of Glenn Hoddle, Clive Allen, Garth Crooks, Steve Perryman, Paul Miller, Graham Roberts, Ray Clemence, Milija Aleksic, Tony Parks and Keith Burkinshaw, to name but a few.

The run of success that these players and manager generated in winning the FA Cup twice in succession in 1981 and 1982 as well as the UEFA Cup in 1984 proved to be the third 'Glory, Glory' eras of my growing up in Tottenham. The second was of course between 1970-71 and 1973-74 when Spurs won the League Cup twice in 1971 and 1973 and the UEFA Cup in 1972 and were UEFA Cup runners-up in 1974. Without any disrespect to that early-seventies side, I believe the team of the eighties were infinitely more talented and exciting to watch. I have to confess that I have two special reasons for fondly remembering those players of the eighties. The first was the enjoyment of taking my young family to Brookfield Lane and White Hart Lane to watch them train and play. The second was when they won the FA Cup on my 30th birthday on Thursday 27 May 1982 in a replay against Queens

Park Rangers. Although not unique, I'm sure I must belong to a select group of Spurs supporters to hold that distinction.

My time in Tottenham came to an end in March 1985 when we bought a house in Cheshunt. I was looking forward to moving out of inner London and being nearer to my sister Pat and brother Alf, who had both been living there for many years, not to mention the added bonus of being less than a mile from Brookfield Lane and the Spurs. Happy days indeed! However, the happy days were not to last for long. Within less than a year not only had my wife left me and the kids, but the Spurs sold the Brookfield Lane training ground. My world had crashed around me. Once again life became difficult for the next few years, during which time I divorced and secured custody of my kids. But, like many years before, happy days were to return. Looking back to those two distressing incidents, I was once later asked how long it took me to come to terms with the set-backs. I replied, 'I still miss that Spurs training ground!' For the record, in 1952 Spurs had originally bought the 11 acres of land in Brookfield Lane for £35,000 and more than 30 years later reportedly sold it for £4million.

During the next few years my son Karl had joined a local junior football team and in time I was asked to take over the coaching and then the managing of the team. Little did I know it then, but this commitment was to ultimately result in my meeting one of my all-time heroes from the 60s. At the end of the 1989-90 season our club (which had a number of different age group sides) had arranged an end of season awards function. One of the other managers had arranged for a Spurs reserve player, whom he had known personally, to attend and present the boys with their awards. A couple of days before the function, it transpired that the player in question would be unable to attend which threw the club's plans into a bit of a panic. I suggested a possible solution which was a bit of a gamble on my behalf. I knew that Cliff Jones lived less than half a mile from my home and I had, on a few occasions, exchanged a few 'Good mornings' over the years, not being one to pester famous people in their private lives. I decided to take my son with me and called at Cliff Jones' home. To my delight Cliff came to the door and I explained my involvement in junior football and the predicament our club found ourselves in. Cliff immediately invited my son and me in and took us into his study, which was clearly his trophy-room, and said he would be delighted to attend our awards function. Cliff then proceeded to not only show my son his various medals and caps, but actually allowed him to hold his 'Double' League winners' medal. Our awards function took place on 15 June 1990 and I had researched Cliff's career in depth as part of my introduction to him as he came to the stage. I believed that I had excelled myself in my efforts to convey Cliff's outstanding achievements. To my horror, Cliff thanked me and said, 'Ron has clearly done his homework into my career but he has forgotten to mention my most important achievement…' I wondered what on earth I could possibly have omitted? Cliff then went on to say '…and something I think is very important to boys of your age…' My mind was frantically trying to fathom out my embarrassing blunder when Cliff concluded '…in all my career I was never booked!' Bugger, sorry Cliff! Needless to say, the rest of evening was an absolute success and was reported in the local newspaper the following week. Later in the year my second wife gave birth to our daughter Kirsty to complete my family and we have all continued to live happily in Cheshunt ever since.

I have one other reason to be grateful for that chance encounter with Cliff Jones, who is without doubt, one of the world's true gentlemen – he was kind enough in 2007 to write an introduction to my first venture into the world of writing called 'Larry

Dilworth and the Legends of Football', which also included a foreword by Jimmy Hill.

In recounting many of the greatest matches that I was privileged to witness over the next 60 years I think it is only right to recall possibly one of the most important and entertaining matches in the history of the club. A match that as a six-year-old, not only did I not witness, but was at the time extremely aware of the tremendous excitement that this result caused in the Tottenham area. I am of course referring to Bill Nicholson's first match as manager.

On Saturday 11 October 1958 the 'Spurs' crowd were assembling on the terraces to the news that Manager Jimmy Anderson had resigned and first team coach Billy Nicholson, who had joined the club as a professional in 1938, had accepted the job of manager with the team lying 16th out of 22 in the old First Division table. Everton, the visitors, occupied the third from bottom position. What was about to happen in the following 90 minutes is probably the greatest start to any managerial career in the history of the game.

SPURS 10 EVERTON 4

Alf Stokes opened the scoring for Spurs before Everton's Jimmy Harris struck an equaliser. Two more Spurs goals from Bobby Smith and George Robb gave the Lilywhites an early 3-1 lead. Then Spurs simply ran riot with three more first half goals from Smith, Stokes and Terry Medwin to go in at half-time 6-1 ahead. The buzz of excitement in the crowd during the interval can only be imagined. Early in the second half Harris scored Everton's second goal, but any hopes of a revival for the visitors was soon quashed when Smith and Tommy Harmer took the score-line to 8-2. Harris then completed his hat-trick, but Smith went one better by scoring his fourth and Spurs' ninth goal of the match. Bobby Collins scored a fourth goal for Everton before centre-half Johnny Ryden scored Spurs' tenth. At the end of October the clocks went back one hour from British Summer Time (BST) to Greenwich Mean Time (GMT) – a good many Spurs supporters may well have considered this (G)oodison (M)en (T) hrashed month. The remainder of the season was one of mixed fortunes with the team finally finishing safe from relegation in 18th position. At the time of the Everton match our family, as previously mentioned (minus Dad of course) had moved and were living just a few miles down the road in a three-bedroom maisonette at number 49 Turner Avenue, off West Green Road, However, what I didn't know then, was that the Spurs 'Glory Glory' years were literally just around the corner.

Gallery

Illustrations by Dennis Alveranga

Bill Nicholson and Keith Burkinshaw

Dave MacKay

Cliff Jones

John White

Bobby Smith and Maurice Norman

Danny Blanchflower

Pat Jennings

Cyril Knowles

Alan Gilzean

Jimmy Greaves

Martin Peters

Garth Crooks

Steve Archibald

Ossie Ardiles

Glenn Hoddle

Graham Roberts

Gary Mabbutt

Chris Waddle

Teddy Sheringham

HOLSTEN

HOLSTEN

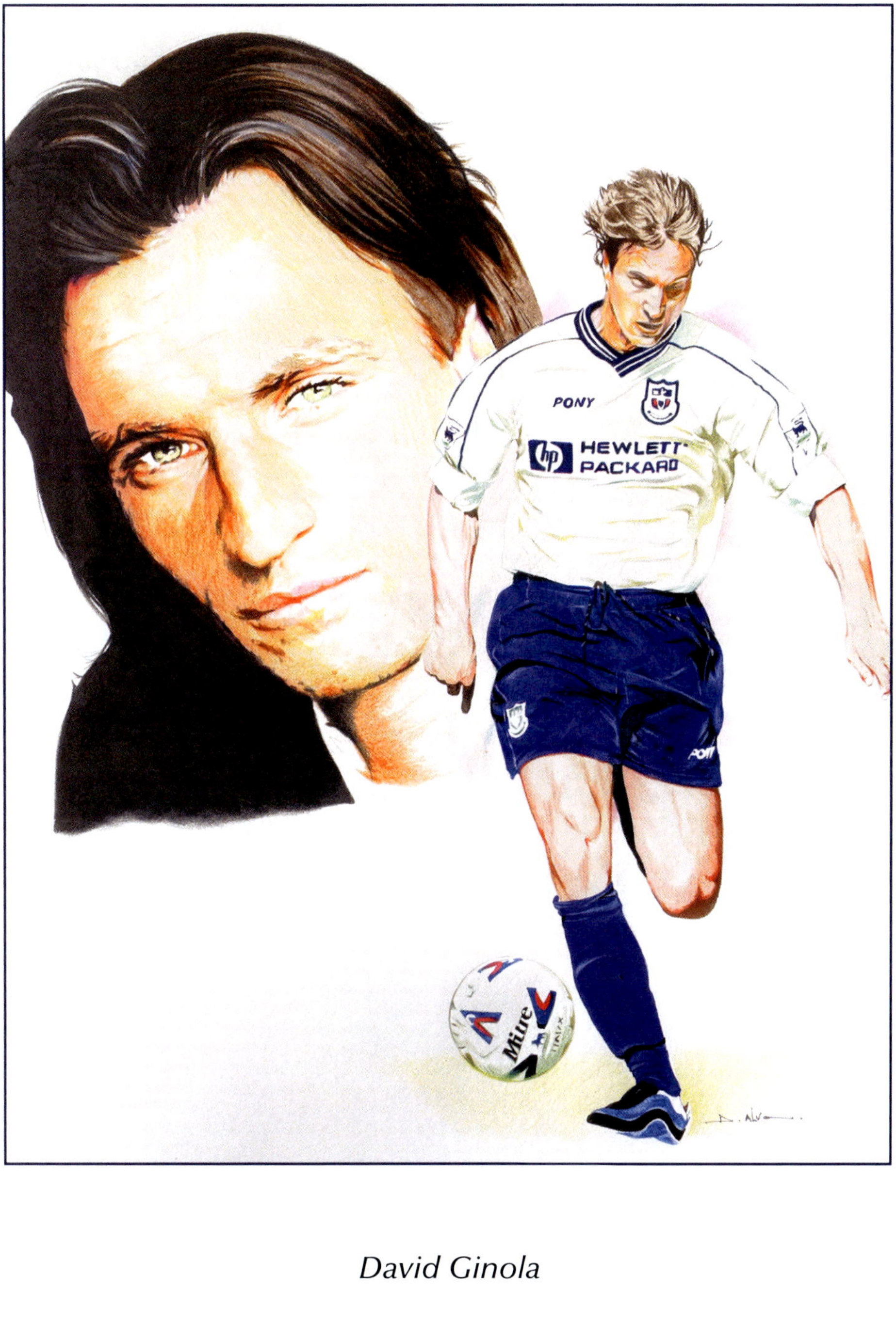

David Ginola

Paul Gascoigne

The start of the 'Double' and the Glory, Glory years

Coincidence plays a large part in football and Everton again figured in the Spurs record-breaking 1960-61 season by being beaten 2-0 at White Hart Lane in the opening game of the campaign. As is now well chronicled, this was followed by another ten straight victories that included a 4-1 thumping of Manchester United and 6-2 demolition of Aston Villa at the 'Lane' with a 3-2 win over Arsenal at Highbury in between. If an extra 'cherry' on the cake was needed to complement this incredible season, the bonus 'Double' was also completed when Arsenal were spanked 4-2 in front of a 65,251 crowd in January. Two extra helpings of icing were added when West Ham United were beaten 2-0 at White Hart Lane on Christmas Eve and 3-0 at Upton Park on Boxing Day, to be later followed by Chelsea being beaten 4-2 at the 'Lane' on Good Friday and 3-2 at Stamford Bridge on Easter Monday. Like I said earlier… 'Happy Days'.

The then record-breaking 11 straight wins at the start of a season came to an end with a disappointing 1-1 draw at home to Manchester City. This was followed by a further four straight wins with the team scoring 16 goals accounting for Nottingham Forest and Newcastle United both conceding four goals on their home grounds, and Cardiff City and Fulham conceding three and five goals respectively at White Hart Lane. Sheffield Wednesday inflicted the team's first defeat by two goals to one at Hillsborough on 12 November. This set-back was quickly brushed off when Birmingham City were crushed 6-0 at White Hart Lane seven days later. In all, Spurs scored 115 goals, winning 31 games, drawing four and amassing a record equalling 66 points. An extra coincidence to this amazing season was that the League title was secured with a win over Sheffield Wednesday (the team that had inflicted the Lilywhites' first defeat) at home in April. A repeat of what had happened in season 1950-51 when Tottenham Hotspur won their first league championship.

The FA Cup success started with a third round 3-2 victory over second division Charlton Athletic at White Hart Lane on 7 January 1961. Three weeks later Spurs were paired with fourth division Crewe Alexandra in round 4 for the second year running. Crewe were beaten 5-1 but this was a far more respectable score-line than the 13-2 trouncing they had suffered the previous season in a replay after gaining a creditable 2-2 draw on their own ground. The fifth round draw saw Tottenham travel to fellow First division Aston Villa and gain a comfortable 2-0 victory. Sunderland, also of the second division, were to be the next obstacle in the sixth round at Roker Park. Despite taking a first half lead, Spurs were suddenly forced to defend for all they were worth when Sunderland equalised early in the second half. A 1-1 draw then saw Tottenham win the replay with ease 5-0. In the semi-final at Villa Park the defending League champions Burnley stood between Spurs and a place in the Final. Burnley posed a real threat to Tottenham having beaten them 4-2 at Turf Moor in the league and pulling back a four goal deficit at White Hart Lane to draw 4-4. This time, however, Burnley were brushed aside 3-0. The Final played at Wembley on 6 May saw Spurs complete the 'Double' with a hard fought 2-0 victory over Leicester City.

As previously mentioned, one of the early, and best results of the 'Double' season, came with the visit of Manchester United. It should be pointed out here that in those days football clubs were mainly supported by local people unlike the present-day and ever-growing band of 'glamour club groupies' who have no association with the geographical area of 'their' team. Which leads me to repeat an often-quoted jibe of the day which was: 'Why do Manchester United supporters prefer watching 'their team' play in London?' Answer: Because there is no travelling involved! Nowadays of course with the game being beamed around the globe, this includes clubs from countries all over the world including Spurs.

TOTTENHAM HOTSPUR 4 MANCHESTER UNITED 1

Saturday 3 September 1960 saw a crowd of 55,442 pack the White Hart Lane terraces. Spurs were top of the table with eight points from four straight wins (at the time only two points were awarded for a win), while United occupied fifth from bottom with just two points after three games. The match was only six minutes old when Bobby Smith opened the scoring. Thirteen minutes later and Les Allen had added a second. United's poor start to the season looked set to continue and they must have feared being dead and buried by half-time. However, things suddenly began to look a whole lot brighter for the visitors when Captain Dennis Viollet pulled a goal back two minutes from the break. In the second half Spurs began to exert constant pressure on the United defence and after 65 minutes Les Allen added his second of the match to take the score-line to 3-1. Bobby Smith, who had scored a hat-trick against Blackpool at the Lane the previous Wednesday, scored his second of the match five minutes from the end to secure a comfortable victory.

I have selected and included the details of the following eight matches, which I feel best convey many of the team's most outstanding performances during the season:

ARSENAL 2 TOTTENHAM HOTSPUR 3

September 10, 1960 saw Highbury Stadium packed as a crowd of 60,088 anticipated a mouth-watering North London derby. With just 12 minutes on the giant clock, a long up-field pass by Les Allen was volleyed home by Frank Saul scoring his first goal of the season. Ten minutes later a throw-in by Dave MacKay was nodded on by Saul for Terry Dyson to head home to give Spurs a 2-0 half-time lead. Spurs fans were clearly looking forward to a comfortable second half. However, on the hour, Herd reduced Arsenal's deficit and just four minutes later Arsenal were level when right half Ward scored with a fierce 25-yard drive. Arsenal fans were sure that the tide was now turning in their favour, but with 19 minutes to go Spurs delivered the killer blow when captain Danny Blanchflower passed to Allen who lobbed keeper Kelsey.

TOTTENHAM HOTSPUR 6 ASTON VILLA 2

September 24, 1960: a huge crowd of 61,356 assembled in the hope of witnessing their team become the first team in League football to win its opening ten games. They only had to wait six minutes for the first goal. A brilliant move between Baker, Blanchflower and Jones ended with White scoring with a wonderful volley. After 14 minutes, White curled a cross-cum-shot to the far post and when Smith charged the Villa keeper Sims, the ball sailed into the net for White's second goal of the match. In the 27th minute Sims was unable to hold a stinging Mackay low drive, and Smith following up had a simple tap in. On the half hour White chipped the ball to Dyson who scored with his left foot to send Villa in 4-0 down at half-time. In the second half Les Allen increased the lead even further. Spurs then appeared to become a bit too casual, and Villa pulled back two quick goals. Dave Mackay rounded off a record-breaking afternoon five minutes from time by volleying home Spurs' sixth goal of the match.

NEWCASTLE UNITED 3 TOTTENHAM HOTSPUR 4

October 29, 1960: in a pulsating game the St James' Park roar after 33 minutes was deafening when centre-forward Len White put the Geordies 1-0 ahead. This lead lasted for only two minutes with centre-half Maurice Norman heading home a Terry Dyson cross. One minute later and Newcastle were back in front when Len White seized on a miskick by Norman to draw the goalkeeper and slip his shot past Bill Brown, only to see full back Ron Henry helping the ball over the line in his attempt to intercept. Newcastle were good value for their 2-1 half-time lead. John White soon levelled the scores for a second time before a 58th-minute goal by Cliff Jones put Spurs 3-2 ahead. Newcastle were not ready to lie down and just four minutes later Hughes saw his hopeful cross elude Keeper Brown and cross the line. What looked like being an even and entertaining drawn match was turned on its head when centre-forward Bobby Smith scored Spurs' fourth and winning goal.

TOTTENHAM HOTSPUR 4 BURNLEY 4

December 3, 1960: Burnley, the reigning champions, gave Spurs the run-around for the first 15 minutes in the pouring rain and any hopes of the home side taking their opponents' crown was looking as damp as the White Hart Lane pitch. The crowd of 58,000, mainly Spurs supporters, were subdued and conscious that this could be the defining examination of their season so far. Then came an incredible three-minute spell. Maurice Norman headed home on 18 minutes. Two minutes later Cliff Jones put Spurs 2-0 ahead. A second goal by Jones just one minute later saw Burnley reeling 3-0 down after just 21 minutes. Worse was yet to come for Burnley when Dave Mackay made it 4-0 after 36 minutes. John Connelly pulled a goal back for Burnley before the half ended. A slip by Ron Henry early in the second half let Jimmy Robson in to score Burnley's second goal of the match. With half an hour still to play another defensive slip, this time by centre-half Norman, allowed Ray Pointer to score a third goal. Burnley were now rampant and after 77 minutes, what looked like being a heavy defeat for the champions, was turned into possibly one of the greatest come-backs and matches ever seen at White Hart Lane when Connelly swept forward and played a one-two with Robson before slamming home the equaliser. The disappointment of letting a four-goal lead slip was tempered by the realisation that Spurs on their day were more than a match for anyone.

TOTTENHAM HOTSPUR 5 BLACKBURN ROVERS 2

December 31, 1960: 48,742 spectators were bathed in brilliant White Hart Lane sunshine just six days after Christmas. Having already been given the perfect Christmas present of beating West Ham home and away on Christmas Eve and Boxing Day, they were hoping for the perfect end-of-year present before celebrating New Year's Eve. They were not to be disappointed.

Blackburn clearly had no intention of wishing Spurs supporters a happy new year when Douglas ended a weaving dribble by shooting past Bill Brown from 20 yards to go one up after 14 minutes. Spurs huffed and puffed for a further 23 minutes before they equalised when Terry Dyson, despite being fouled, managed to swing over a cross that Bobby Smith chested down and hit a shot that went in off the post. Twelve minutes into the second half another Dyson cross was volleyed home by Les Allen. Two minutes later a third Dyson cross was back-heeled by Smith to Danny Blanchflower, who took the ball in his stride before slipping the ball under the Blackburn goalkeeper. Two more goals from close range by Allen and Smith gave Spurs a 5-1 lead. Blackburn had played well but could only score a second consolation goal.

TOTTENHAM HOTSPUR 4 ARSENAL 2

January 21, 1961: 65,251 spectators filled the Lane to watch the second North London derby of the season. Arsenal were looking to reverse the 3-2 defeat they had suffered at Highbury earlier in the season and things looked promising when Henderson spun and fired a low shot into the corner of the Spurs net. Within 15 minutes, however, Spurs were in front. First John White put Les Allen through on the left to score with an angled shot, then Terry Neill tripped Terry Dyson in the box and Danny Blanchflower converted from the penalty spot. Dave Mackay and Peter Baker exchanged passes before Mackay sent Cliff Jones away to set up Bobby Smith for a simple tap-in. Early in the second half, Jones had a shot which was charged down and found its way to Allen who made no mistake in scoring Spurs' fourth goal. A cross from Haverty was diverted into the Spurs net to end the scoring and complete the double over their closest neighbours.

TOTTENHAM HOTSPUR 4 CHELSEA 2

March 31, 1961: an eager crowd of 65,032 were packed tightly inside White Hart Lane for the first of the two Easter London Derby games. Spurs were simply far too good for their West London neighbours and easily established a four-goal lead. Chelsea's only hope at the commencement of the match was that their star goal-scoring machine Jimmy Greaves would turn the Spurs defenders inside out and run riot. However, half back Tony Marchi had other ideas and completely subdued the little wizard. Cliff Jones grabbed two goals, Les Allen and young Frank Saul one apiece. Two late goals by Brabrook and Tinall in the last minute gave the score-line a respectability it hardly deserved.

TOTTENHAM HOTSPUR 2 SHEFFIELD WEDNESDAY 1

April 17, 1961: 61,205 fans had assembled on the terraces at White Hart Lane for an evening match played under floodlights that would serve to illuminate not only this magnificent stadium but the team that would be crowned Champions of England just 90 minutes later. Sheffield Wednesday were second in the table six points behind Spurs, both having played 38 games. However, nobody in the ground, including the Spurs players, expected an easy match and so it was to prove. Don Megson blasted Wednesday into a 27th minute lead which left Goalkeeper Bill Brown well beaten. Two goals in the last three minutes of the first half were enough to win not only the match but the League Championship. The first was scored by Bobby Smith who lobbed the ball over Peter Swan the Wednesday centre-half before running around him to smash the ball home. The second was scored by Les Allen who seized on a knocked down header by centre-half Maurice Norman from a Danny Blanchflower free-kick to rifle a right foot volley into the net. This match will be remembered for the determination of the Spurs to play football against a Wednesday side that were clearly happy to use rough tactics in a bid to derail their closest rivals. How fitting it was for Les Allen to score the goal that clinched the Championship just a month before becoming the proud father of Clive Allen, on 20th May. Clive would also go on to wear the Spurs colours with pride and in season 1986-87 he scored a record 49 goals in all competitions.

After the 'Double'

The following season would see the team strengthened by the signing of Jimmy Greaves from A C Milan for a fee of £99,999. The reason for this strange figure was because Manager Bill Nicholson decided that he didn't want his latest signing to be burdened with the tag of being the first one-hundred-thousand-pound footballer in British football. Spurs supporters were understandably excited at the prospect of a second consecutive league title, or perhaps incredibly, another 'Double'?

Despite beating Arsenal 4-3 and Chelsea 5-2, and a Jimmy Greaves inspired debut hat-trick 5-2 thumping of Blackpool in between, all at White Hart Lane, Spurs finished the season in third place, four points behind the champions Ipswich Town, who were managed by Alf Ramsey. Ramsey was of course Spurs' full-back who made 40 appearances alongside Billy Nicholson in the 1950-51 championship winning team. Spurs were not to be denied when it came to the FA Cup, however. A 3-1 semi-final crushing of Manchester United at Hillsborough was followed by Burnley being beaten at Wembley by the same score-line. The team also acquitted themselves with pride before falling at the semi-final stage of the European Cup.

Season 1962-63 would see Tottenham Hotspur create yet another landmark achievement when they became the first British side to win a major European trophy when they beat holders Athletico Madrid 5-1 in the European Cup Winners' Cup. In the league, Everton were the only side above Spurs at the end of the season despite the following four outstanding performances:

Aug 25: West Ham United 1 Tottenham Hotspur 6. Goalscorers: Medwin, White, Greaves 2, Jones, Lyall og.

Sept 29: Tottenham Hotspur 9 Nottingham Forest 2. Goalscorers: Medwin, White, Allen (pen), Greaves 4, Jones 2.

Oct 24: Tottenham Hotspur 6 Manchester United 2. Goalscorers: Medwin 2, Greaves 3, Jones.

April 15: Tottenham Hotspur 7 Liverpool 2. Goalscorers: Jones 2, Saul, Greaves 4 (1pen).

The following three seasons saw the team struggle to maintain their momentum.

Season 1966-67 saw the last of the great 'Double' stalwarts, captain Dave MacKay, lead the side to yet another FA Cup triumph when Chelsea were beaten at Wembley 2-1 with goals by Jimmy Robertson and Frank Saul, who as a 17-year-old, also made six league appearances in 1960-61.

The Start of the Eighties Glory, Glory years

It's somewhat debatable when, exactly, did the Eighties Glory, Glory years begin? Was it July 1967 when 16-year-old Steve Perryman signed as an apprentice? Was it in April 1974 when another young apprentice called Glenn Hoddle signed for the club? Was it in July 1976 when Keith Burkinshaw was promoted to team manager? Or perhaps in June 1978 when two of Argentina's World Cup winning team called Osvaldo Ardiles and Ricky Villa arrived in N17? Conversely, maybe it was in May 1980 when a 21-year-old called Graham Roberts was signed from non-league Weymouth for a mere £30,000?

One thing is for sure, all of the above combined to produce the vision, class and power that produced the most exciting Spurs team since the sixties.

Football is of course a matter of much debate and conjecture, not to mention personal opinion. Spurs' league performances and positions during this time did little to justify my comparison to the sixties successes, but I based my assertion on the individual brilliance of so many players who on their day could truly be described as 'World class'. Sadly, the one thing collectively they could not be described as was 'Consistent'. This was most definitely the era of 'Cup' success with flashes of brilliance and exciting football that had been so lacking during the seventies.

1980-81 continued the tradition of Spurs winning a trophy when the year ends in one.

14 MAY 1981: FA CUP FINAL REPLAY, WEMBLEY: TOTTENHAM HOTSPUR 3 MANCHESTER CITY 2.

Archibald and Crooks combined, as they were to do so often in other games, to cause City a real headache at the back. Tony Galvin's runs stretched City's defence allowing Hoddle, Ardiles and Villa the space to make telling passes and runs. Whilst at the back for Spurs, Steve Perryman, Graham Roberts, Paul Millar and Chris Hughton were, as usual, solid and resolute. Milia Aleksic was powerless to stop City's two goals. And who could ever forget Ricky Villa's amazing dribble that ended with what has been described as the greatest Cup Final winning goal of all time? Villa and Crooks both having scored earlier in the match.

27 MAY 1982: FA CUP FINAL REPLAY, WEMBLEY: TOTTENHAM HOTSPUR 1 QUEENS PARK RANGERS 0.

Just like the season previously, Spurs needed a replay to secure their second successive FA Cup victory. There were three changes to the Cup Final team of last season. In came Ray Clemence in goal, Paul Price and the immensely talented Micky Hazard. There were two reasons that prevented Micky Hazard being a permanent first team player, and they were Glenn Hoddle and Ossie Ardiles. Spurs were missing their two Argentine stars Ardiles and Villa due to the escalating Falklands war. This was a game which proved that sometimes you have to grind out a win when not playing well. Glenn Hoddle slotted home an early penalty after Graham Roberts had been tripped in the box after making one of his trademark rampaging, swashbuckling runs. In the league Spurs finished fourth as they would also do the following season.

23 MAY 1984: UEFA CUP FINAL, SECOND LEG, WHITE HART LANE: TOTTENHAM HOTSPUR 1 ANDERLECHT 1.

The first leg of the final in Brussels was also drawn 1-1. Paul Miller had opened the scoring for Spurs with a 57th minute header before a late equaliser from Olsen, five minutes from time, left the tie all square and set-up an exciting second leg in London. Spurs would again be without the injured Ray Clemence and Glenn Hoddle, but now found themselves further weakened by the absence of inspirational captain Steve Perryman due to suspension after picking up a booking in the first leg. The replay was a nervous affair for both teams and after a goal-less first half the 46,258 crowd were stunned when Anderlecht, the current holders, went ahead with a goal from Czerniatynski on the hour. Spurs now kicked into overdrive and began pounding the Anderlecht goal, but it was only when Ossie Ardiles came off the substitute's bench that they looked like finally finding their way through the resolute Anderlecht defence. In the 84th minute Ardiles managed to hit the bar from close in following a corner and the rebound was picked up by captain-for-the-night Graham Roberts who stormed his way through the crowded penalty box to hammer home the equaliser. After 90 minutes with the scores still level, the game went into extra-time. Both teams had chances to win the game but failed to take them, and the final was to be decided by a penalty shoot-out. Graham Roberts strode forward to take and score the first of four successful spot-kicks, and with the score at 4-3 to Spurs, Anderlecht had one more chance to level the scores. Gudjohnson stepped up and watched in horror as Tony Parks pulled off a spectacular save to the deafening roar of the crowd. Manager Keith Burkinshaw, who had decided to leave at the end of the season due to a dispute with the club, collected his third trophy in four years and become the club's second most successful manager after Bill Nicholson. One wonders how much more could have been achieved by this collection of immensely talented players if Keith had stayed anywhere near the 16 years given to Bill Nicholson.

18 MAY 1991: FA CUP FINAL, WEMBLEY: TOTTENHAM HOTSPUR 2 NOTTINGHAM FOREST 1.

The eighties drew to a close for Spurs with another FA Cup Final appearance in 1987. The team was, by now, much changed and only Glenn Hoddle and Ossie Ardiles remained from the successful side at the beginning of the decade. Despite their efforts, and the free-scoring, record-breaking Clive Allen, Spurs lost to Coventry City 2-3 after extra-time. Now, with the year ending in one, Spurs were back. Despite going a goal down and almost immediately losing Paul Gascoigne, Spurs re-organised and began to fight back. Spurs' luck, however, seemed to be deserting them. Gary Lineker had a goal (later proved to be wrongly) disallowed for offside and then saw his penalty saved by Crossley, the Forest keeper. However, ten minutes into the second-half, Paul Stewart levelled the scores. As in 1987, the final again went to extra-time and would be decided by an own goal. This time, unlike the wicked deflection by poor Gary Mabbutt against Coventry, Des Walker was to suffer the same fate to take the cup back to White Hart Lane.

In conclusion

It is, of course, almost impossible to name a greatest Spurs XI when, like myself, you have been lucky enough to have seen so many wonderful players over the years. Apart from those already mentioned in the earlier pages of this book I include a few more players, in no particular order, that have graced White Hart Lane.

Alan Gilzean, with Jimmy Greaves (known as the G-Men), Martin Peters, Cyril Knowles, Phillip Beal, Pat Jennings, Alan Mullery, Chris Waddle, Paul Gascoigne, Teddy Sheringham, Jurgen Klinsman, David Ginola, Gareth Bale and the latest... Harry Kane, who hopefully, still has so much more to contribute?

I'm sure that you, the reader, could add a good many more.

Author's Hall of Fame

Having recently celebrated my 70th birthday, and researched and reviewed the careers of the vast number of hugely talented and influential personalities that have represented THFC in the history of the Club, I have decided to recognise the following two individuals (one, a manager, the second, a player) with an Award of Distinction for the greatest contribution to the Club.

Bill Nicholson OBE

William Edward Nicholson served the Club for 55 years as player, coach and manager, having joined THFC in 1938. But it was during his 16 years as manager that Bill Nicholson catapulted the 'Spurs' to the heights never before or since seen. Between 1958 and 1974 Tottenham Hotspur won eight trophies and Bill became the first English manager to win the 'Modern' Double of League Champions and FA Cup winners in 1961, which most people at the time thought to be impossible, and followed this by becoming the first British manager of a British club to win a European trophy (the European Cup Winners' Cup) in 1963. It is also to Bill's credit that he combined being not only immensely successful but modest, hard-working and respected throughout not only the Club but the football world in general.

Steve Perryman MBE

Stephen John Perryman spent 17 years as player and Club captain during which time he became the most successful trophy-winning player in the history of THFC in the form of two UEFA Cups, two FA Cups and two League Cups. Steve continues to hold the record of most appearances for the Club and this distinction was achieved when appearances meant playing a full 90 minutes in the days of only one substitute and not for coming on for the last few minutes of a match as in the modern era of three and five subs. To amass the amount of appearances that Steve did clearly means that he was immensely vital to the successful squads of the early 70s and 80s, which is no mean feat when you consider the calibre of players he was competing with. Like Bill Nicholson, Steve was hard-working, dedicated, loyal and respected. More importantly Steve was home-grown (an original, One of our Own), not an already established star purchase. Consider the value Steve represented to the Club in light of some questionable, recent, vastly expensive short-term purchases.

When I close my eyes I can still see Bobby Smith thumping home goals with both headers and shots, or Jimmy Greaves gliding past defender after defender before passing the ball into the back of the net. Pat Jennings plucking the ball out of the air with one hand and Steve Perryman scoring two screamers against A C Milan, not forgetting Glenn Hoddle chipping and volleying goals from every angle of the pitch, as well as Graham Roberts crashing home the equaliser against Anderlecht that ultimately led to Spurs winning the UEFA Cup in 1984 after Tony Parks saved the last penalty shoot-out kick.

Those were the days!

Family Album

Author and big brother Alf, Turner Avenue circa 1959

Big sister Pat with boyfriend Mick's old banger.
Turner Avenue 1962

Mum with baby brother Robert, sister Pat,
niece Tina and nephew Paul. Turner Avenue 1968

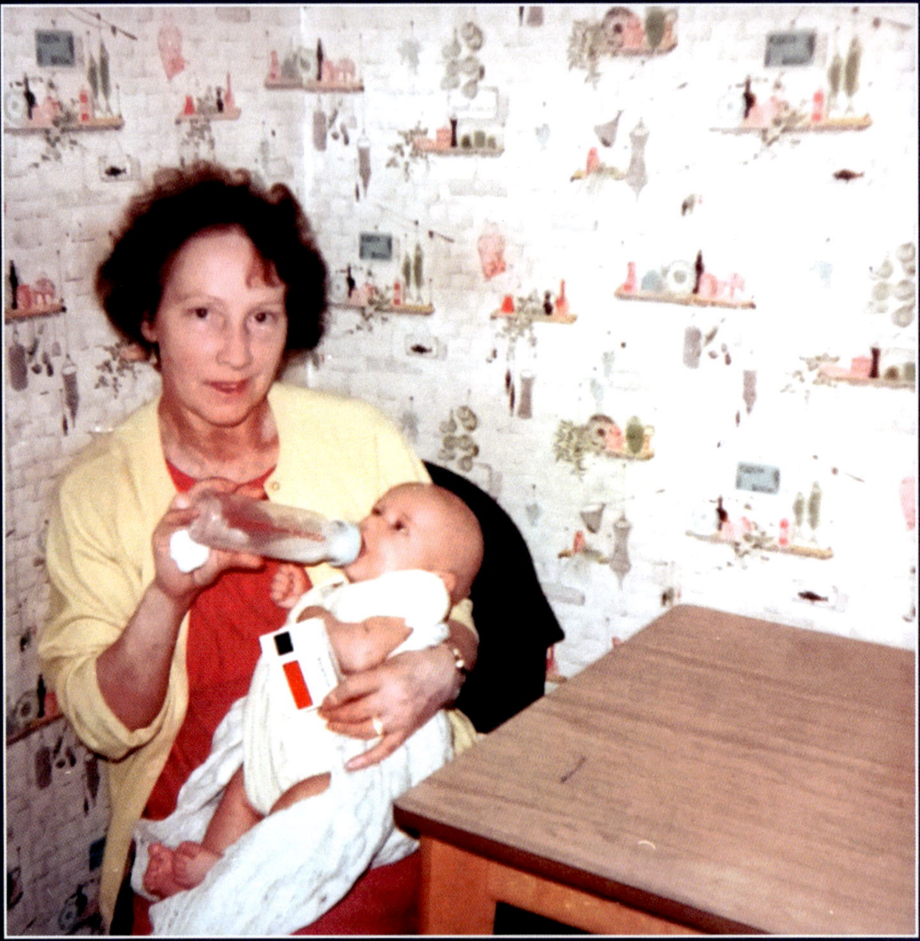

Mum and baby Robert. Packet of Guards 'fags' at the ready. Turner Avenue 1968